ROSWELL

This series features unsolved mysteries, urban legends, and other curious stories. Each creepy, shocking, or befuddling book focuses on what people believe and hear. True or not? That's for you to decide!

45th Parallel Press

Published in the United States of America by Cherry Lake Publishing
Ann Arbor, Michigan
www.cherrylakepublishing.com

Reading Adviser: Marla Conn MS, Ed., Literacy specialist, Read-Ability, Inc.
Book Designer: Felicia Macheske

Photo Credits: © photoBeard/Shutterstock.com, cover; 21; © Dennis van de Water/Shutterstock.com, 5; © Arman Zhenikeyev/Shutterstock.com, 7; © John D Sirlin/Shutterstock.com, 8; © Rommel Canlas/Shutterstock.com, 11; © turtix/Shutterstock.com, 13; © chippix/Shutterstock.com, 15; © M. Cornelius/Shutterstock.com, 16; © sdecoret/Shutterstock.com, 18; © Beckie/Flickr, (CC BY 2.0), 22; © MagicMore/Shutterstock.com, 24; © 9foto/Shutterstock.com, 27; © jgolby/Shutterstock.com, 29

Graphic Elements Throughout: © iofoto/Shutterstock.com; © COLCU/Shutterstock.com; © spacedrone808/Shutterstock.com; © rf.vector.stock/Shutterstock.com; © donatas1205/Shutterstock.com; © cluckva/Shutterstock.com; © Eky Studio/Shutterstock.com

45th Parallel Press is an imprint of Cherry Lake Publishing.

Library of Congress Cataloging-in-Publication Data

Names: Loh-Hagan, Virginia, author.
Title: Roswell / by Virginia Loh-Hagan.
Description: Ann Arbor : Cherry Lake Publishing, [2017] | Series: Urban legends. Don't read alone! | Includes bibliographical references and index.
Identifiers: LCCN 2017001044 | ISBN 9781634728980 (hardcover) | ISBN 9781634729871 (pdf) | ISBN 9781534100763 (pbk.) | ISBN 9781534101654 (hosted ebook)
Subjects: LCSH: Unidentified flying objects—Sightings and encounters—New Mexico—Roswell Region—Juvenile literature.
Classification: LCC TL789.5.N6 L64 2017 | DDC 001.94209789/43—dc23
LC record available at https://lccn.loc.gov/2017001044

Cherry Lake Publishing would like to acknowledge the work of The Partnership for 21st Century Skills. Please visit *www.p21.org* for more information.

Printed in the United States of America
Corporate Graphics

TABLE OF CONTENTS

Chapter One

CLOSE ENCOUNTERS OF THE STRANGE KIND

What did Kenneth Arnold see? What did William Woody see? What did Dan Wilmot see? What did Mac Brazel see?

Kenneth Arnold flew planes. He flew around Mount Rainier, Washington. Arnold saw nine flying objects. This happened on June 24, 1947. The objects flew in a V shape. They were bright and shiny. They flew quickly. They moved like **saucers** skipping across water. Saucers are small plates. This inspired the term *flying saucers*. Arnold's sighting started the age of the **UFO**. UFO means unidentified flying object.

Newspapers reported the story. Some people believed Arnold. They said they also saw UFOs.

The U.S. Air Force didn't believe Arnold. They said he saw a **mirage**. Mirages are things that people think they see but that aren't really there.

There were 16 other UFO sightings supporting what Arnold saw.

CONSIDER THE EVIDENCE

The U.S. Air Force studied UFO sightings. The study was called Project Sign. It started in 1948. Project Sign became Project Grudge. This happened in 1949. Then, it became Project Blue Book. This happened in 1952. It was the longest U.S. government study of UFOs. Project Blue Book collected over 12,000 UFO sightings. Over 90 percent were "identified." This means they were caused by something known. About 6 percent were "unidentified." This means the cause was unknown. Project Blue Book ended in 1969. This mission had two goals. One was to see if UFOs were a threat. Another was to analyze UFO information.

There were two other important sightings. They happened soon after Arnold's sighting.

Dan Wilmot owned a business. He lived near Roswell, New Mexico. He was with his wife. He was sitting on his front porch. He saw a bright flying saucer. He saw it move at high speeds. He said it was 20 feet (6 meters) across. He saw glowing lights. The lights zoomed across the sky. This happened on July 3, 1947. This happened at night. This happened in 40 to 50 seconds.

William Woody was also outside. He saw a bright object. He saw it crash. This happened on July 4, 1947.

Wilmot's wife heard a swishing sound.

There was a bad thunderstorm before Brazel's sighting.

On July 7, 1947, Mac Brazel saw the **wreckage**. Wreckage is what remains after a crash. It's the trash.

Brazel worked on a ranch. He checked on his sheep. He saw strange pieces of an aircraft. He heard about Arnold's UFO sighting. He thought a UFO crashed. He saw pieces of a "flying disk." He saw metal sticks taped together. He saw foil chunks. He took pieces to his shed. He showed neighbors. The neighbors said it was an alien spaceship. Brazel told the sheriff. The sheriff told the Roswell Army Air Force base. Then, soldiers came. They took the pieces away.

Chapter Two

GROUND ZERO FOR UFOs

What are the different types of close encounters? What is special about Roswell?

Arnold and Brazel had close **encounters**. Encounters are meetings. Close encounters have different types. There are close encounters of the first kind. This is the sighting of a UFO. But there's no proof. There are close encounters of the second kind. This is a UFO sighting that has proof. Proof can be pictures. There are close encounters of the third kind. This is when direct contact is made. Humans have contact with aliens. There are close encounters of the fourth kind. Examples are **abductions**. To abduct means to kidnap. Some people believe aliens have kidnapped them.

Some people think aliens take humans for experiments.

SPOTLIGHT

BIOGRAPHY

Ray Santilli lives in London. He made a video. He showed three government people in suits cutting open a dead alien. He said it was an alien from Roswell. He said a military official gave it to him. He did this in 1995. The film was 17 minutes long. It was in black and white. It was seen by many people. It was on TV. In 2006, he admitted to staging the film. He hired someone to make a fake alien from lamb bones. But he still said the film was true. He said it was based on a real video. He said he saw the real video. He said the real video got damaged. He said he included some of the real frames.

Roswell is famous for its close encounters. It's known as **ground zero** for UFO research. Ground zero means starting point.

It's most famous for the 1947 UFO **incident**. Incident means event. The crash site was 75 miles (121 kilometers) from Roswell. But soldiers from the Roswell Army Air Field took the wreckage. They brought it to their base.

Roswell is important for the military. It's home to bases. In 1941, it was a military training center. It trained bomber crews. It was a flying school. Roswell also has a missile range. It has a **nuclear** weapons lab. Nuclear means special power source.

Roswell has museums about UFOs.

Chapter Three

THE 1947 UFO INCIDENT

What happened after Brazel reported the wreckage? What is the role of the RAAF in the Roswell incident?

George Wilcox was the sheriff. He was surprised by what Brazel found. He contacted the RAAF. RAAF means the Roswell Army Air Field. Wilcox talked to Major Jesse Marcel. Marcel investigated. He drove out to the ranch. Marcel said something must have exploded and fell from the sky. He said pieces were all over. He said pieces covered a wide area. He collected the wreckage. He said, "Never saw anything like it."

Officials at the RAAF made a statement. The *Roswell Daily Record* was a newspaper. It put the story on the front page. The headline was, "RAAF captures flying saucer on ranch in Roswell region."

Many newspapers picked up the story.

UFO sightings rely on people's eyewitness stories.

Roger Ramey was a brigadier general. He examined the wreckage. He said it was a weather balloon. He showed reporters pieces. He showed foil, rubber, and wood. The *Roswell Daily Record* reported a correction. This happened the next day. People lost interest in Roswell.

Glenn Dennis was a **mortician**. Morticians handle dead bodies. He said the RAAF called him. He said the RAAF asked for small sealed coffins. He said they asked how to **preserve** bodies. Preserve means to save. Dennis said he went to the base hospital. He saw wreckage pieces. He saw strange writing. Then, military police kicked him out.

UFO-logy is the study of UFOs.

Dennis talked to a nurse. The nurse saw "several, small non-human bodies." She drew pictures. She was sent away. No one saw her again.

Stanton Friedman studies UFOs. He revived interest in the Roswell incident. This started in 1978. He interviewed hundreds of people. He talked to anyone connected to Roswell. He talked to Marcel. Marcel told him the wreckage wouldn't burn. He said it weighed nothing. He said it wouldn't bend.

Friedman thinks an alien spaceship crashed. He thinks there were alien bodies. He thinks the government covered up everything. He made people interested in Roswell again.

REAL-WORLD
CONNECTION

Roswell hosts a party for UFO fans. They host the Roswell UFO Festival. Thousands of people attend. They dress up as aliens. The festival celebrates what happened at Roswell. It's a four-day event. It takes place in late June and early July. There are guest speakers. There are authors. There are live shows. There are costume contests for humans and pets. There's an electric light parade. There's music. There are food trucks. There are many more activities. Everything has an alien theme. Light posts are shaped like alien heads. Restaurants are shaped like flying saucers.

Chapter Four

ALIENS VS. GOVERNMENT

What are some ideas about Roswell?
How is Roswell a government cover-up?

Many people don't believe the weather balloon story. They think the government hides secrets.

Some people think the government is making top secret weapons. The United States was worried about Russia. People think the U.S. government used alien power to make weapons against Russia.

Some people think the government made a mistake. The government lost a weapon. It didn't want the public to know. So, it distracted people. It let people believe in aliens. This kept people away from the truth.

Some people think the government was holding Japanese prisoners of war. The government experimented on the prisoners. It made weapons. UFOs are cover stories.

There are many books and movies written about Roswell.

Charles Berlitz and William Moore studied Roswell. They interviewed over 90 people. They think an alien spaceship flew over New Mexico. Then, it got hit by lightning. This killed the aliens. The U.S. government hid them. They also swapped the wreckage. They got rid of the alien spaceship. They added weather balloon scraps instead.

Some people think there were alien bodies found in Roswell. The bodies were there for several days. Animals had eaten some organs. The bodies were 4 to 5 feet (1.2 to 1.5 m) tall. They had big heads. They had large eyes. Their mouths look like slits. They were thin. They had long arms. They had four fingers.

People create images of aliens based on sightings.

INVESTIGATION TIPS

- Talk to people who believe in aliens. Ask them if they've seen aliens. Ask them if they've made contact with aliens.

- Read about aliens. Read people's stories about seeing aliens. Learn more about aliens.

- Read science fiction stories. Watch science fiction movies. Figure out what's based on science.

- Visit Roswell. Take a trip to the city. Go to the International UFO Museum and Research Center. Go to the Roswell Museum and Art Center.

- Visit a military base. See what happens there.

- Study space travel. Learn how rockets work. Learn about space.

- Track what you see in the sky. Record any strange flying objects.

Some people said they saw four aliens at Roswell.

Some people think the government studied the bodies. The government kept these aliens top secret. No one was allowed to talk about it. But some people talked. A captain said he saw the bodies. Another officer said he guarded the storage site. UFO researchers believe them. They don't trust the government. They want to believe aliens are real.

The government won't admit anything. Government officials deny aliens. They don't want to scare people. They don't want people to panic. They don't want people to feel threatened. UFO researchers think the government is lying.

Chapter Five

THE BORING TRUTH

What is the problem with sightings? What is Project Mogul? What are dummy drops?

UFO researchers interviewed hundreds of people. There are problems with people's stories. Not everyone can be trusted. Only a few people really see anything. Most people repeat what they hear.

The government's story is more boring than aliens. But many believe it's the truth. The government said Roswell is part of Project Mogul. This project detected sound waves. It looked for Russian bombs. It flew microphones on balloons. It was top secret. The weather balloon was a cover story. The government admitted the truth years later. It said the Roswell crash was a Project Mogul balloon.

People believe what they want to believe.

EXPLAINED BY SCIENCE

Some people report being stolen by aliens. They report being experimented on. Scientists don't think this is true. They blame "sleep paralysis." Paralysis means not being able to move. Some sleepers think they're being watched. They feel scared. They can't move. Their ears ring. Their chests feel tight. They can't breathe. They feel themselves leaving their bodies. They feel pain. Sleep paralysis is a disorder. It's when the brain disconnects from the body. This happens right before a person falls asleep. Or it happens right before a person wakes up. It affects half of all people at least once.

What about the alien bodies? The government blamed crash test **dummies**. Dummies are fake bodies. These dummies were 6 feet (1.8 m) long. They had rubber skin. They had metal bones. They didn't have any features. They looked like alien bodies.

The Air Force did "dummy drops." They did this over military bases. They did this over empty fields. These were experiments. Pilots tested ways to survive falls. They're high in the sky. They dropped dummies. Then, military cars picked up the dummies.

Real or not? It doesn't matter. The Roswell incident lives in people's imaginations.

Some people think the dummies are a cover story.

DID YOU KNOW?

- There was another UFO crash. It happened in Aztec, New Mexico. It happened in 1948. It was fake. The incident is sometimes called "The Other Roswell."

- Orson Welles had a radio show. He based it on a science fiction book. The book is *War of the Worlds*. Welles told people that aliens were invading Earth. Many people listened to the show. They believed him. This happened in 1938.

- MUFON stands for Mutual UFO Network. It investigates UFO sightings. It's a group for civilians. Civilians are people who are not military. They're not scientists. CUFOS is the Center for UFO Studies. MUFON and CUFOS are the top UFO groups.

- Jimmy Carter was a U.S. president. He reported seeing a UFO. This happened in 1969. This happened in Leary, Georgia.

- Betty and Barney Hill said aliens kidnapped them. They said they were taken to a UFO. This happened in 1961. They said the aliens had gray skin. They called them "Grays." Some people think "Grays" and Roswell aliens are at Area 51. Area 51 is a Nevada Air Force base. It's believed to have top secret files. It's believed to have proof of aliens.

- Edward Ruppelt was a U.S. Air Force officer. He came up with the term UFO. He did this in 1952.

CONSIDER THIS!

Take a Position: Do an Internet search about aliens. Some people think aliens are not real. Some people think they are real. What do you think? Argue your point with reasons and evidence.

Say What? Many people visit Roswell. Research the city. Explain why Roswell is a tourist destination. Explain what visitors can do there. Explain what visitors can see there.

Think About It! Read the 45th Parallel Press book about Roanoke Colony. The colonists disappeared. Some people think aliens kidnapped the colonists. There are many strange things that happen. Some things are hard to explain. So, why do people blame aliens?

LEARN MORE

- Halls, Kelly Milner, and Rick C. Spears (illustrator). *Alien Investigation: Searching for the Truth About UFOs and Aliens*. Minnetonka, MN: Millbrook Press, 2012.

- Higgins, Nadia. *Area 51*. Minnetonka, MN: Bellwether Media, 2014.

- Krull, Kathleen, and Chris Santoro (illustrator). *What Really Happened in Roswell? Just the Facts (Plus the Rumors) About UFOs and Aliens*. New York: HarperCollins, 2003.

GLOSSARY

abductions (ab-DUHKT-shuhnz) kidnappings

dummies (DUHM-eez) fake bodies; mannequins

encounters (en-KOUN-turz) meetings

ground zero (GROUND ZEER-oh) starting point

incident (IN-sih-duhnt) event

mirage (muh-RAHZH) something that appears to be real but is not

mortician (mor-TISH-uhn) a professional who handles dead bodies

nuclear (NOO-klee-ur) special power source

preserve (prih-ZURV) to save

saucers (SAW-surz) small plates, usually for cups

UFO (YOO EF OH) unidentified flying object

wreckage (REK-ij) what remains after a crash; trash

INDEX

ABOUT THE AUTHOR

Dr. Virginia Loh-Hagan is an author, university professor, former classroom teacher, and curriculum designer. She has become a fan of science fiction, especially *Star Wars*. She lives in San Diego with her very tall husband and very naughty dogs. To learn more about her, visit www.virginialoh.com.